You're Not Going Out Like That!

Paul Cookson lives in Redford with Sally, Sam, Daisy and Lightning the guinea pig and spends most of his time visiting schools to perform his poems and lead workshops.

He likes to wear loud shirts, colourful socks and blue suede shoes (and sometimes a pair of big red underpants) while doing this. If he could he would also wear a top hat with mirrors on, an Everton scarf and a Batman cape but if he did his family would probably say . . . 'You're not going out like that!'

Sam Hearn lives in an anorak in Richmond, south-west London and he loves drawing pictures. He lives with his favourite pair of jeans, four cardigans and a very loyal three-year-old pair of blue pants.

Other books by Macmillan

DON'T GET YOUR KNICKERS IN A TWIST
Poems chosen by Paul Cookson

HA HA: POEMS TO MAKE YOU LAUGH
Poems chosen by Paul Cookson

WHAT SHAPE IS A POEM?
Poems chosen by Paul Cookson

THE VERY BEST OF PAUL COOKSON

THE EVIL DOCTOR MUCUS SPLEEN
AND OTHER SUPERBAD VILLAINS
Poems chosen by Paul Cookson

SHORTS!
Poems chosen by Paul Cookson

MY STEPDAD'S AN ALIEN
Poems chosen by David Harmer

You're Not Going Out Like That!

Poems chosen by
Paul Cookson

Illustrated by
Sam Hearn

MACMILLAN CHILDREN'S BOOKS

Dedicated to Kath, Tony and Zak

First published 2003 by Macmillan Children's Books
a division of Macmillan Publishers Limited
20 New Wharf Road, London N1 9RR
Basingstoke and Oxford
www.panmacmillan.com

Associated companies throughout the world

ISBN 0 330 39846 6

1 3 5 7 9 8 6 4 2

A CIP catalogue record for this book is available from
the British Library.

Printed and bound in Great Britain by Mackays of Chatham plc, Kent

Contents

You're Not Going Out Like That!
— Paul Cookson and David Harmer   1

Accessories to Go! — Sue Cowling   3

Some Unexpected 'Wear and Tear' — Trevor Harvey   4

Take a Tip from Me — Graham Denton   5

Men in Tights — Graham Denton   6

Mother's Pride — Damian Harvey   8

A Mother's Despair — Patricia Leighton   10

Flares — Roger Stevens   12

Dad's Secret — Tony Langham   14

Flat and Safe — Coral Rumble   16

Fishy Fashion — David Harmer   18

Seeing Red — Gina Douthwaite   21

Where Shall I Have My Tattoo?
— Redvers Brandling   22

My Headmaster's Ties — Ian Bland   24

What's Wrong Now? — David Harmer   25

Dressing Up – John Coldwell 27

First Stab – Gina Douthwaite 28

Close Shave – Trevor Harvey 29

Cotton Creases – Gina Douthwaite 30

Just Look at Yourself! – Alan Priestley 32

A Hat – Colin West 34

Dorothy Scales – Philip Waddell 36

DIY Tongue-stud – Mike Johnson 37

No Earrings Allowed – Steven Herrick 38

Clothes Conscious – Trevor Harvey 40

My Knickers – Ann Ziety 42

This Autumn, the Well-Dressed
    Witch is Wearing – Dave Calder 44

Euripides – Colin West 46

Bonding – Jill Townsend 47

Why I Am Always Going to Wear
    My Baseball Cap, So There! – David Harmer 48

Out of Season – Paul Cookson 50

Velcro Rap – Trevor Millum 52

Two Pants Turner – Angie Turner 54

School Tie – Roger Stevens   56

Trendsetter – Clive Webster   58

Growing Old Gracefully – Andrew Collett   59

Snubbed – Anne Wright   60

A Time and a Place – Clive Webster   61

Forget It! – Paul Cookson   62

The Real Thing – Patricia Leighton   64

You're Not Going Out Dressed
    Like That! – Dave Calder   68

The Secret Life of Mr Harper – Paul Cookson   70

Take Off that Hat! – Ted Sheu   72

Fashion – Brian Patten   75

Two Witches Discuss
    Good Grooming – John Coldwell   76

Purple Shoes – Irene Rawnsley   79

One Thing in Common – Paul Cookson   82

You're Not Going Out Like That!

What do you think you look like?
You're not going out like that!
Where do you think you're going?
You're not going out like that!
Look at the state of you!
You're not going out like that!
You are an embarrassment!
You're not going out like that!
Fashion! Don't make me laugh!
You're not going out like that!

N – O SPELLS NO
YOU'RE NOT GOING OUT LIKE THAT!
NO WAY JOSÉ
YOU'RE NOT GOING OUT LIKE THAT!

That skirt's a bit too short – **You're not . . .**
Pink hair and dreadlocks – **You're not . . .**
You're falling off those heels – **You're not . . .**
You can see right through that top – **You're not . . .**

And as for you . . . baseball cap, back to front
Training shoes like small canoes
Slipknot hoody top, and as for those new tattoos

1

N – O SPELLS NO
YOU'RE NOT GOING OUT LIKE THAT!
NO WAY JOSÉ
YOU'RE NOT GOING OUT LIKE THAT!

Please, Mum! Please, Dad!
You're not going out like that!
Yes we will – no you won't
Yes we will – no you won't

Please, Mum! Please, Dad!
Don't go out like that!
It's really, really embarrassing, Dad.
Don't go out like that!
How old d'you think you are, Mum?
Don't go out like that!
Please, Mum! Please, Dad!
Don't go out like that!

Paul Cookson and David Harmer

Accessories To Go!

Belt,
Tiara,
Cowgirl hat,
Keyring,
Kerchief,
Neon plait,
Boa,
Scrunchie,
Glitter spray –
Pocket money
Blown away!

Sue Cowling

Some Unexpected 'Wear and Tear'

I've a Liverpool cap,
An Everton tag,
A pendant from Leeds,
A Newcastle bag,
An Arsenal shirt,
A Man U scarf,
Some Chelsea socks
And, for a laugh,
I wore them ALL
When I went out!
That's how my
INJURIES came about . . .

For I'd not realized
I would get
A PUNCH from
Every bloke I met . . . !

Trevor Harvey

Take a Tip from Me

If you want to know what's fashionable
If you want to know what's new
What's hip, what's hop, what's happening
What's trendy and what's cool
If you want to spot what clothes are hot
What's 'in' and what is 'It'
Just look at how your dad is dressed . . .
And do the *opposite*!

Graham Denton

Men in Tights

While Robin Hood
looked rather good,
the Sheriff of Nottingham
was not quite so hot in 'em.

Graham Denton

Mother's Pride

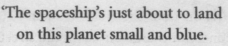

'The spaceship's just about to land
   on this planet small and blue.
         Our attack force is armed and ready
         and just look at the state of you . . .

      'Your tentacles are twisted,
       your claws are in a mess
     and when you combed your nose hair last
   I can only guess.

'Your fangs are in a terrible state,
your breath smells of rotten meat.
And those boots you're wearing are
   so full of holes
I can smell your sweaty feet.

'Your eyes are oozing yellow goo,
your gills are dripping slime.
Getting yourself in such a state
should be made a galactic crime.

'As the door slides slowly open
and you charge off down the street,
we must be the proudest parents
in the whole of the Zargon fleet.'

Damian Harvey

A Mother's Despair

Where's the black lipstick
What's with the blonde hair?
And you've polished your shoes.
What's up? Don't you care?

What's that slip of a skirt
and that silky gold top?
You didn't get those
at 'Weirdo's Top Shop'.

Why not wear that nice jumper,
the one with the holes,
and your big swirly skirt
with the border of mould?

A bit more eyeliner?
More shadow, less sheen?
Those cheeks are too rosy,
brush on this green.

And what's that you're spraying
all over yourself?
Fragrance of Freesias?
Now do have some sense!

Pastel pink nail polish?
Glossy cream tights?
Your dad will go ape!
You'll give grandma a fright.

I'm losing my patience.
Just what are you at?
You look like a freak, a geek,
    a HUMAN
You're not going out like that!

Patricia Leighton

Flares

I wear flares
And am often catapulted
Into the night sky
Where I drift slowly down
My legs brilliantly glowing
Lighting up the town

Roger Stevens

Dad's Secret

My Dad's got a dreadful secret.
A deep, dark secret.
He thinks nobody knows
About it.
He thinks he's the only one.
But I know about it.
Oh yes, I know about it . . .

At least once a week
He creeps upstairs to the attic
And when he thinks
Nobody's watching, he takes
Off his trousers . . .
Then he opens up
This dusty old trunk
And takes out a pair
Of pale blue, flared trousers
Which are straight out
Of the 70s
And puts them on.

Then, in front of an old
Full-length mirror,
While he sings 'Night Fever'
(Very quietly)
He starts to dance . . .

. . . and that's when
I'm going to start videoing
Him the next time he thinks
Nobody's watching.

Tony Langham

Flat and Safe

Mum's had a perm;
Either that or some accident with electricity!
And she likes it.
Her friends like it.
My dad likes it.
But her head looks like an exploding mattress.
She's got more coils than a party full of streamers,
And more bounce than ten kangaroos on trampolines!
She says it makes her feel glamorous.
She says I'll get used to it –
But I won't!
She ought to look like Mum,
The way she always used to look,
Flat and safe.

Coral Rumble

Fishy Fashion

I think
I'd look really smart
with a fish on my head.

Just a smallish one
silver and shiny, like the tinfoil
Mum uses to wrap the turkey
its little fishy eyes closed tight
mouth wide open in a happy grin
tail frozen in a final flick.
Fish like that
are quite cheap from the market
if it gets too tatty
I'll just buy another one
perch it on my head
like a small cap.

Mum and Dad don't agree
they think wearing fish
is a silly idea,
not to mention the smell
they think
my head will go all slimy
and stink of the sea.

I suppose they've got a point,
fish are strongly scented creatures
and you can't always find
a fish that fits
for once I think my parents are right.

I'll go and buy
a frozen chicken instead
that should do the trick.

David Harmer

Seeing Red

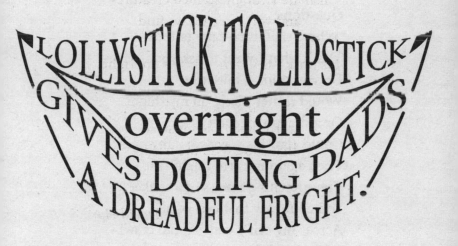

LOLLYSTICK TO LIPSTICK GIVES overnight DOTING DADS A DREADFUL FRIGHT.

Gina Douthwaite

'Where Shall I Have My Tattoo?'

Questions:
'Where shall I have my tattoo?
That's what I want to ask you.
Do you think a butterfly
Would flutter nicely on my thigh?
Or a dragon, deepest black,
Could claw his way across my back?
Then again my arm might take
The stretching sinews of a snake.
You could say that best of all
Across my calf a crab should crawl.
Where shall I have my tattoo?
That's what I want to ask you.'

Answer:
'I suppose they'd all look good,
But do you think you really should?
Why not go for just a tan
After all – you are my gran!'

Redvers Brandling

My Headmaster's Ties

I don't mind his balding haircut
That hasn't changed in twenty years,
I can tolerate the shirts
Bedecked with stains and mucky smears,
I can put up with his trousers
Though they're never the right size,

But why does my headmaster
Have to wear those awful ties?

I've come to terms with all his sandals
And his paisley print cravat,
I've accepted all his waistcoats
And the Russian soldier's hat,
I concede he's gone past caring
And he just won't modernize,

But tell me why he has to wear
Those stupefying ties?

Ian Bland

What's Wrong Now?

I threw away my dirty old jeans
stopped wearing the same football kit
for five weekends in a row
dropped my dirt-encrusted socks
in the washer
changed my incredibly sweaty T-shirt
for a slightly cleaner one
put my horribly humid trainers in the bin
where they ran for five minutes
all on their own
I even had a shower, without being told
to have a shower
and then, after all that
I still got done off my mum
and all I did was borrow
my big sister's hair colouring kit
had a bit of a go
I turned out a very bright shade of orange

which has sort of started
to go green round the edges
nothing wrong there, in fact
rather smart and cool and neat I thought
but oh no
despite all my best efforts
I'm grounded for a week
I tell you what
that's the last time I
decide to smarten myself up a bit
so there!

David Harmer

Dressing Up

I'm tottering around on Mum's new shoes
I'm wearing Dad's work vest
I have my sister's school scarf on
Tied around my chest.

My older brother's PE shorts
Fit neatly on my head
Round my neck is our dog's
lead
That I found in the
shed.

Who do you think I am
supposed to be?
Easy, I'm my
whole family.

*John
Coldwell*

First Stab

How, mascara, to apply?
Stick a stick into an eye,
rub it black and blink it dry,
squint into the mirror. Cry.

Gina Douthwaite

Close Shave

This morning
I had
My first
Shave

I couldn't wait
ANY LONGER
For stubble
To appear.
(I've waited
A year.)

What I think it needs is
ENCOURAGEMENT.

After all, my gran has
A moustache –
So why
Can't I?

Trevor Harvey

Cotton Creases

Cotton creases, satin slithers,
silk will wrinkle, chiffon withers,

wool is spongy, springy, squeezy,
keeping it in shape's not easy,

leather stretches, linen crushes,
flannel, when it's wet just mushes,

felt is fuzzy, lace is holey,
corduroy is ridged and roly,

nylon, in the dark, is sparky,
taffeta is stiff and sparkly,

velvet is as smooth as honey,
Lycra's light as paper money,

denim's coarse and thick and tough, we
can, like canvas, treat it roughly.

Bare skins wore bearskins till moths
made draughty holes – so man made cloths.

Gina Douthwaite

Just Look at Yourself!

Just look at yourself!
You're wearing smart trousers
Instead of your jeans!
And where are your trainers?
Those shoes are clean!
Your shirts tucked in,
Your collar's fastened up.
You no longer look
Your usually mucky pup.

You've washed your hands!
You've washed your face!
And – good heavens – you've even washed
     behind your ears,
Something you've not done for many years!

Your sister looks her usual self,
Wearing what first came to hand off the shelf.
And your dad, you know, won't change his ways;
The clothes he's wearing have all seen better days.
And I haven't had time to do my hair –
And yes, my make-up is a mess, of that I'm
     well aware.

So don't think that you're going out smart
   and dressed like that
When the rest of us look like something that's
   been brought home by the cat!

GO AND GET CHANGED AT ONCE!

Alan Priestley

A Hat

I'm going to the hatter
For to purchase me a hat.
It doesn't really matter
If it's tall or if it's flat.

I don't mind if it's black or brown,
Or if it has a crumpled crown,
Or if the brim is up or down;
A simple hat is all I ask,
To cover up my ears.

I don't ask for a bonnet
That is made of velveteen,
With a lot of ribbons on it
That are yellow, pink or green.

I don't ask for a hat of crêpe,
Or one of an exotic shape,
Or one that's all tied up with tape;
A simple hat is all I ask,
To cover up my ears.

I don't want one with feathers,
Or with cherries ripe and red,
A plain hat for all weathers
Would be fine for me instead.

I do not really mind a bit
If my hat's not a perfect fit,
If I can just get into it,
A simple hat is all I ask,
To cover up my ears.

Colin West

Dorothy Scales

Dorothy Scales
Peruses the rails
Always to admire
The 'On Sale' attire.

Last spring's latest shirt
And last summer's skirt,
Last autumn's suits
And last winter's boots.

Dorothy Scales
Peruses the rails –
Clothes are her passion
But *after* a fashion.

Philip Waddell

DIY Tongue-stud

Theeth inthtruchthionth
can't be wight:
I DIYd thith
tongue thtud
late latht night –
when I woke
my mouth wath leaking
and thith ith how
I thtarted thpeaking.

Mike Johnson

No Earrings Allowed

The new Principal
addressed the school assembly today
and told us the new rule.
No earrings allowed on boys or girls.
The next day
Peter Mitchell from Year 6
arrived at school
without his Nike earring,
but he did have a nose-stud.
The new Principal
addressed the school assembly
and told us the new rule.
No nose-studs allowed.
The next day
Peter Mitchell arrived
without his nose stud.
He had a mohawk haircut.
At assembly
The new Principal said
No mohawks allowed.
The next day
Peter Mitchell arrived at school
without a mohawk.
His head was shaved

to a prickly stubble.
He charged 5 cents to anyone
who wanted to feel it.
(It felt like my dad's face
when he hasn't shaved.)
Peter also wore really cool sunglasses.
At assembly
The Principal said
No sunglasses allowed.
The next morning
two hundred and twenty-one students
without earrings, nose-studs, mohawks
and sunglasses stood by the front gate
waiting for Peter Mitchell to arrive.
He was absent, sick.
We waited at assembly,
expecting the Principal
to say
Children are not allowed to get sick.

Steven Herrick

Clothes Conscious

With my pink shirt and blue shoes,
My green and yellow socks,
My mauve scarf and orange hair
I felt GREAT, I walked on air!
People frowned – but did I care?
And soon I saw what made them stare . . .
I was outside – in my *underwear*
(White, unwashed, a bit threadbare!) –

No wonder there were frowns and snorts –
For I forgot to wear my *shorts*!

Trevor Harvey

My Knickers

My knickers are enormous
My knickers are supreme
They cover nearly all of me
In lovely bottle-green

The gusset's made of iron
The waist is made of plastic
And Martin Cooper likes to twang
Their re-inforced elastic

Compared to other knickers
My knickers are the best
They reach to well below my knees
And just above my chest

My knickers are so versatile
And truly heaven-sent
For when I go out camping
I use them as a tent

My knickers are unusual
And sometimes for a change
I like to wear them on my head
Which looks a little strange

Once travelling on a cruise ship
Which sank just off Peru
We used my knickers as the boat
For passengers and crew

My knickers are remarkable
And have a special function:
To be as big as Birmingham
Without Spaghetti Junction

Completely indestructible
With girders round the back
They can withstand a hurricane
Or nuclear attack

Recognized by royalty
For quality and size
My knickers have been knighted
They've won the Nobel Prize

Though other knickers come and go
And fall along the way
My knickers are immortal
My knickers never fray

Ann Ziety

This Autumn the Well-Dressed Witch is Wearing . . .

The House of Horror holds a Hallowe'en show
where all the dark and midnight hags
gather to gawp at the new sad rags
and ghouls go all gooey and drool
at the latest shrouds
as flimsy and pale as clouds.

A wax model stands stiff, stuck with pins,
in a shocking pink pointed hat –
you hear one zombie say to another
'I wouldn't be seen dead in that!'

Ghosts glide down the black catwalk
past werewolves dressed to kill,
but the see-through look's no thrill
to goblins in their birthday suits
feathered hats and scarlet boots

And trendy witch magazine writers
who're scribbling with their quills
gloat and note with fixed smiles
that this year it's good news for ravers:
after the long flowing merlin style

the cutty sark is back in fashion –
essential gear for the new passion
of extreme bonfire-leaping or
that wild party in the woods.

But there's plenty on show for
the more mature, haute couture
gruesome garments, dismal dresses
trimmed with bat-wings and bat-messes;
the undead this season will be wearing
slime green and mould grey with a hint of mud
delicately flecked with blood
and if you want to get admirers staring
accessorize, yes, accessorize
with a tasteful necklace of rabbits' eyes
or handbag of newt skin.

Some vampires say it's hardly worth rising for
but you can't please every old thing
and it's so much fun in the graveyard, darling,
how I wish you were here!

Dave Calder

Euripides

Euripides, Euripodoze,
You always rip your Sunday clothes.
Euripodoze, Euripides,
You always rip them at the knees.

Colin West

Bonding

A chink of rings,
a clank of chain.
Kath and her boyfriend
are snogging again.

Eyebrows, ears,
nose and chin:
there isn't much
room left for skin.

But all of a sudden
Kathryn cries, 'Ow!'
Their rings
have interlocked somehow

and even though
they start to row
they'll have to stay
together now.

Jill Townsend

Why I Am Always Going to Wear My Baseball Cap, So There!

My baseball cap is rammed on tight
Wear it all day, wear it all night
Wear it to school, wear it to bed
It's always there, stuck on my head.

Got a peak at the front, strap at the back
Started off white but it's almost black
Fixed firm and fast for three months now
Can't get it off no way, no how.

What happened was, it stuck really well
I used superglue instead of gel
Plastered my hair with gooey sludge
Now the baseball cap just won't budge.

My mum's upset, as for my dad
Just the other day he got so mad
He tugged really hard, flipping heck
He nearly pulled my head off my neck.

Grandad attacked it with some shears
I nearly lost both my ears
Grandma lathered my head with soap
Then tried to drag it off with a rope!

Been smeared in lard, grease and tar
Washing up liquid, oil from the car
They've yanked my head until it's sore
But the cap's still stuck for evermore.

I don't care much what people say
My cap is cool, I like it this way
Here's a fashion tip, let me share it
If the cap fits, I'm going to wear it!

David Harmer

Out of Season

At the Christmas party, resplendent in black cape and fangs,
Dad stands underneath the mistletoe as Dracula
To no avail.

At Easter the chocolate tends to stain the white beard
And red suit that Dad insists on wearing
When he comes down the chimney.

On the beach he's always the centre of attention.
Well, you would be in the middle of summer
In a giant, furry bunny outfit digging holes to hide
    melting eggs in.

And at Hallowe'en he truly frightens everyone
When he arrives in just his swimming trunks –
The brown ones that reach his knees with the
    yellow dots on
(the trunks that is, not his knees).

That's the trouble with Dad.
He's always behind the times.

Paul Cookson

Velcro Rap
(for three voices, if available)

my coat does up
with buttons
  my coat does up
  with a zip
  my coat does up
  with velcro
    and gives
      a perfect grip
      my coat is cosy
      all buttoned
        my coat is zipped
      to my chin
      my coat is done up
with velcro
but it's hard
to get
  all of me in . . .

        my coat undoes
          with buttons
            my coat undoes
        with a zip

my coat undoes
with velcro
   with a wonderful
   rippety-rip –
   yeah!
   a wonderful
   rap
 rippety
rip!

Trevor Millum

Two Pants Turner

I'm Two Pants Turner and I'm so cool.
I'm Two Pants Turner and I make the girls drool.
I'm Two Pants Turner and I like to groove.
I'm Two Pants Turner you should see me move.

I woke late one morning, everyone was in a flurry.
And my dad got me dressed in a bit of a hurry.
Well you see, my dad is a right old fool
He gave me two pairs of pants to put on for school.

CHORUS

Since that day I think it's really brill.
Wearing two pairs of undies, giving the girls a thrill.
When I strip for P.E. the girls start to giggle.
So I turn around and give them a wiggle.

One pair red and the other pair green.
It's the grooviest sight you've ever seen.
Now it seems that I'm everybody's friend.
Since I started off the latest trend.

CHORUS

Angie Turner

School Tie

The school rules state clearly
That the tie must be worn
Right length, tied neatly
It's the school uniform.

So we all wore it short,
Halfway up to our chests.
Then loose, like a scarf,
I liked that style best.

For a few days we tied it
As tight as we dare
Until Sam couldn't breathe
And fell off his chair.

We held competitions
Who could make their knot fattest
And we unpicked our tie
To see whose could be tattiest.

Tho' the school rules say clearly
How the tie should be worn
We are all individuals
We refuse to conform.

Roger Stevens

Trendsetter

The teacher had a new dress on,
A sort of bright vivid red.
'Well, boys and girls, does it suit me?'
'Oh yes, sir,' the boys and girls said . . .

Clive Webster

Growing Old Gracefully

Our mum's acting very strangely
it's something we can't bear,
she's started to wear my sister's clothes
and do strange things with her hair.

She's even sending little notes
to Dad when he's alone,
and is always out at parties
and never off the phone.

She's using words like 'hip' and 'cool',
which she's never done before,
she's started sitting on Dad's knee
or a beanbag on the floor.

Mum's acting very strangely
we don't know what to do,
for she hasn't been the same
since turning forty-two!

Andrew Collett

Snubbed

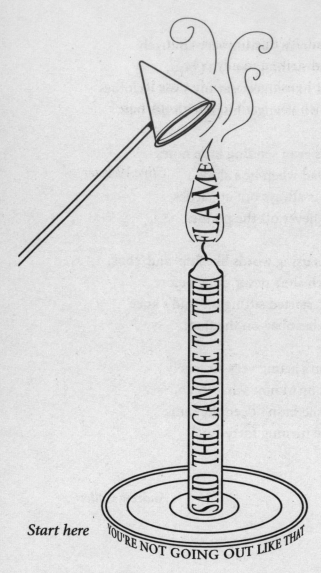

SAID THE CANDLE TO THE FLAME

Start here YOU'RE NOT GOING OUT LIKE THAT

Anne Wright

A Time and a Place . . .

'Dad, it's fine to wear a kilt,
And strike a manly pose.
But I wish you wouldn't use it
When you want to blow your nose . . .'

Clive Webster

Forget It!

I don't care if it is dark and no one will see
I may want walkies . . . but not that badly

If you insist on wearing that baggy purple jumper
with the patches on the elbows
and those yellow tracksuit bottoms
with the holes in the bum
and your Carlisle United bobble hat
with those tattered tartan slippers
you can forget it!

I'm staying – and that's final
I'd be a laughing stock in the park

No way
I wouldn't be seen dead with you looking like that

Said Foo Foo the manicured poodle.

Paul Cookson

The Real Thing

'Gran, you didn't wear that!'

'*I did*,' she said.

'But it's almost up to your . . .'

'*Backside*,' she said. '*Well,
I had a decent one then*.'

'Love the beads,' I said,
'but they're hanging down to my knees!'

'*Daft brush!*' she said. '*Here, tie a knot
in them, halfway down, like this*.'

'Gran, no one could dance in these –
look at those pointed toes, those heels.'

'*We did*,' she sniffed. '*Girls still had
a bit of deportment back then*.'

'De-what?'

'*Never mind*,' she said.

'I don't believe it!' I said, pulling something
long and blonde from the box.

'*My hairpiece*,' she giggled. '*Six shillings
for styling at Mo's Hair Salon.
A good match. My hair used to be
the exact same colour as yours.*'

I fished through the tissue in case
there was something I'd missed, drew out
an old photo of Gran in this gear and . . .

'*Your granddad*,' she said, '*at the firm's
New Year's Dance. That's where we met.*'

I could see it was him.
Grandad with sleeky smooth hair,
shiny suit, white shirt.
Same eyes, same grin.

'*Well*,' she said, '*do you want to borrow this stuff
for your school sixties disco or not?*'

'I don't know . . .'

'*Course you do! No use to me in this box.*
Come over early. I'll alter the dress,
get the hairpiece done, pin it up just right.'

You should have seen me:
peacock blue mini dress
(frill round the neck, no sleeves)
turquoise pearl beads
black patent shoes
(they fitted, looked great)
and my hair, high and smooth,
held in place with a black velvet band.

'*Dance one for me,*' said Gran
as I made for the door.

'I promise,' I said.

And all night
I rocked, twisted and jived
Gran's memories and dreams
under moving, glitter ball circles
of diamond-bright light.

Patricia Leighton

You're Not Going Out Dressed Like That!

You're not going out dressed like that!
That ring's too big for your nose
and what with zips, chains and safety pins
you're wearing more metal than clothes.

You've not going out dressed like that!
That T-shirt's a filthy disgrace –
what did make those stains? Its so short and tight
you pop out all over the place.

You're not going out dressed like that!
Red hot pants don't suit you, they're sad,
and those three-inch high heels just look silly –

go back upstairs and change, Grandad!

Dave Calder

The Secret Life of Mr Harper

At school he's just the coolest teacher
Dressed in his designer best
The mums all think he's really great
The dads are not impressed.

He knows about the latest bands
And all the PlayStation Games
Knows everything on Pokemon,
Can tell you all their names.

Yes Mr Harper's ace
Mr Harper's cool
Wicked, hip and up to date
The coolest guy in school.

But see him at the weekend
down the railway station
You won't believe your eyes
At the transformation.

A knitted blue and yellow scarf
An orange large cagoule
A pair of flares, brown corduroy . . .
He doesn't seem so cool.
A duffel bag that's stuffed with crisps
A pair of thick rimmed glasses
Binoculars for peering at
Any train that passes.

A thousand pens for writing down
The numbers in his jotter,
Mr Harper's secret . . .
He's really a trainspotter.

Paul Cookson

Take Off that Hat!

No son of mine is going out
with *that* thing on his head!
Don't take another step young man . . .
Did *you* hear what I said?

I cannot let you leave this house.
Please take it off this minute!
You shame our famous family name
when *that* has your head in it.

It looks like stuff the cat drags home
returning from a prowl.
At least your friends won't *laugh* at you –
they'll only hoot and howl!

The colours are ridiculous,
the style is bizarre.
Why you could join the circus,
and be their hottest star!

A clown of clowns, the best around –
the kids would race to see you.
But if you asked them, honestly,
they'd rather *die* than be you.
So do not *dream* of going out –
I simply couldn't bear it.
Besides, that hat is *mine*, you know,
And I would like to wear it.

Ted Scheu

Fashion

I dye my hair bright green,
Unless I shave it clean.
I wear a wig upon my nose
And bright earrings on my toes.
And though I know my legs are pylons
I wear such pretty nylons.
Every day upon my shirt
I dab a little grease and dirt.

(Though I'm the brightest kid in the class
and my brain is more than ample
Teacher says she thinks I'm weird
And set a bad example.)

When people stop and say,
'Why do you have that on?'
I smooth down my little dress and say,
'It is the latest fashion.'
All the girls adore me,
They do not think I'm a fool.
They smile and say, 'Our Billy's
The best-dressed boy in school.'

Brian Patten

Two Witches Discuss Good Grooming

'How do you keep your teeth so green
Whilst mine remain so white?
Although I rub them vigorously
With cold slime every night.

'Your eyes are such a lovely shade
Of bloodshot, streaked with puce.
I prod mine daily with a stick
But it isn't any use.

'I envy so, the spots and boils
That brighten your complexion.
Even rat spit on my face
Left no trace of infection.

'I've even failed to have bad breath
After eating sewage raw,
Yet your halitosis
Can strip paint from a door.'

*'My dear, there is no secret,
Now I don't mean to brag.
What you see is nature's work
I'm just a natural hag.'*

John Coldwell

Purple Shoes

Mum and me had a row yesterday,
a big, exploding
howdareyouspeaktomelikethatI'mofftostayatGran's
kind of row.

It was about shoes.
I'd seen a pair of purple ones at Carter's,
heels not too high, soft suede, silver buckles;
'No' she said.
'Not suitable for school.
I can't afford to buy rubbish.'
That's when we had our row.

I went to bed longing for those shoes.
They made footsteps in my mind,
kicking up dance dust;
I wore them in my dreams across a shiny floor,
under flashing coloured lights.
It was ruining my life not to have them.

This morning they were mine,
Mum relented and gave me the money.
I walked out of the store wearing new purple shoes.
I kept seeing myself reflected in shop windows
with purple shoes on,
walking to the bus stop,
walking the whole length of our street
wearing purple shoes.

On Monday I shall go to school in purple shoes.
Mum will say no a thousand furious times
But I don't care.
I'm not going to give in.

Irene Rawnsley

One Thing in Common

A vicar in his spotted knickers
A footballer in yellow flippers
A rock star in his fluffy slippers
Batman dressed up as a cat
A soldier in an evening dress
A nun in just a stringy vest
A tutu on a diplomat . . .
They're not going out
like that

A ballet dancer in hobnail boots
A teacher in their birthday suit
A judge in just a thong (minute)
A cricketer without a bat
A dad in Mum's best mini skirt
A mum in Dad's worst sweaty shirt
A diving suit on an acrobat . . .
They're not going out like that

A rapper with no baseball cap
Dracula not dressed in black
Santa with a rubbish sack
They're not going out like that!
A cowboy with a pink cravat
The Queen in just her
    plastic mac
The Lone Ranger
    – no mask and hat
They're not . . .
        going out . . .
            like that!

Paul Cookson

THE TEACHER'S REVENGE

Poems chosen by Brian Moses

In an average classroom, in an average town, on an average afternoon it is not only the pupils who are staring at the clock longing for the bell to ring. The teachers are waiting too . . .

The Pupil Control Gadget

Science teacher Robert West
built a gadget, which, when pressed
caused consternation far and wide
by zapping pupils in mid stride.
It froze all motion, stopped all noise,
controlled the rowdy girls and boys,
and on fast forward was great fun.
It made then get their schoolwork done,
their hands a blur, their paper smoking,
with teachers cheering, laughing, joking.
And on rewind, (that too, was nice)
you could make them do their schoolwork twice.
Robert, now a millionaire,
is selling gadgets everywhere.
Timid teachers, pupil bossed
pay cash and never mind the cost.

Marian Swinger

taking my human for a walk

Poems chosen by Roger Stevens

Ever wondered what your pets think of you?
Taking My Human for a Walk reveals the truth at last!

A Sticky Riddle

It might seem obvious to you humans
But it puzzles me every day
If he wants the stick so badly
Why does he throw it away?

Roger Stevens

A selected list of titles available from Macmillan Children's Books

The prices shown below are correct at the time of going to press. However, Macmillan Publishers reserve the right to show new retail prices on covers which may differ from those previously advertised.

Title	Author	Price
My Stepdad Is an Alien	David Harmer	£3.99
The Teacher's Revenge	Brian Moses	£3.99
Are You Sitting Comfortably?	Brian Moses	£3.99
Taking My Human for a Walk	Roger Stevens	£3.99
What Shape Is a Poem?	Paul Cookson	£4.99
Scottish Poems	John Rice	£4.99
Bet You Can't Do This!	Sandy Ransford	£3.99
Revolting Jokes	Sandy Ransford	£3.99

All Macmillan titles can be ordered from our website, www.panmacmillan.com, or from your local bookshop or are also available by post from:

Bookpost
PO Box 29, Douglas, Isle of Man IM99 1BQ

Credit cards accepted. For details:
Telephone: 01624 836000
Fax: 01624 670923
E-mail: bookshop@enterprise.net
www.bookpost.co.uk

Free postage and packing in the UK.
Overseas customers: add £1 per book (paperback) and £3 per book (hardback).